One World, One Heart

Susan Polis Schutz

Designed and Illustrated by
Stephen Schutz

Blue Mountain Press™
SPS Studios, Inc., Boulder, Colorado

To order this book, please phone or e-mail SPS Studios, publishers of Blue Mountain Arts® products. Let us know the quantity of books you want and how you are going to distribute them. The books are packed 100 books per carton, so please order in this increment.

This book promotes understanding, peace and tolerance for all people. We want to distribute millions of copies FREE throughout the world, but we need your help to do this. We hope readers will listen to this author's message.

E-mail: oneworldoneheart@spsstudios.com

Phone: 303-417-6404

Copyright © 2001 by Stephen Schutz and Susan Polis Schutz.

All rights reserved. No part of this book may be reproduced in any manner whatsoever without written permission from the publisher.

The following poems by Susan Polis Schutz have appeared in previous Blue Mountain Arts® publications: "We need to feel more...." Copyright © 1972 by Continental Publications. "Love is...," "When you interact with children...," and "A friend is...." Copyright © 1981, 1982, 1984 by Stephen Schutz and Susan Polis Schutz. All rights reserved.

ISBN 0-88396-631-X

Certain trademarks are used under license.

Manufactured in the United States of America
Fourth Printing: February 2002

This book is printed on fine quality, laid embossed, 80lb. paper. This paper has been specially produced to be acid free (neutral pH) and contains no groundwood or unbleached pulp. It conforms with all the requirements of the American National Standards Institute, Inc., so as to ensure that this book will last and be enjoyed by future generations.

 This book is printed on recycled paper.

SPS Studios, Inc.

P.O. Box 4549, Boulder, Colorado 80306

INTRODUCTION

We all hear the same sounds. We look up and see the same sky. We cry the same tears. Our feelings and emotions are the same. All mothers are sisters. All fathers are brothers. All children are one.

Yet there is hate. There is violence. There is intolerance. There is confusion among people. We don't try hard enough to understand each other. We don't seem to realize that we all have the same basic needs, no matter who we are or what part of the world we come from.

We must understand the differences among us and celebrate the sameness. We must make the world a place where love and friendship dominate our hearts. Equality, respect, compassion and kindness must guide our actions. Only then will we all be able to peacefully and lovingly live the life we each choose.

Susan Polis Schutz

One moon
One sun
One world
One heart

We need to feel more
to understand others
We need to love more
to be loved back
We need to cry more
to cleanse ourselves
We need to laugh more
to enjoy ourselves

We need to be honest and fair
when interacting with people
We need to establish a strong ethical basis
as a way of life
We need to see more
than our own fantasies
We need to hear more
and listen to the needs of others
We need to give more
and take less
We need to share more
and own less
We need to realize the importance of the family
as a backbone to stability
We need to look more
and realize that we are not so different from one another

We need to create a world where
we can trust one another
We need to create a world where
we can all peacefully live
the life we choose

We all cry the same tears
tears of fright
tears of sadness
tears of loss
tears of frustration
tears of disappointment
tears of loneliness
Lands are flooded with our tears
We need one another's
kindness, cooperation, trust and respect
to survive

We must talk
until there are no more words
We must explain
until everything is understood
We must be honest
until nothing is hidden
We must listen
until everything has been said
We must question
so that we know why
We must be fair
so that everyone's basic needs are met
If there is no communication
there will be no bond
If there is no bond
there will be no friendship

Nothing Should Divide Us

We who inherit the earth
  who cheer the new moon peaking
    through the womb
  who admire the green leaves of summer
    turning to lustrous reds and yellows
  who watch them fall to the ground
    cold, brown and stiff...

We who give birth to new life
  who are exhilarated by the sun rising
  who are romanced by the sun setting
  who dream to the floating clouds...

We who have a passing mark on the future of the world
  must have the same heart
  must have compassion for one another
  must have respect for one another
  must understand that though we have differences
    we all want the same things
Nothing should divide us

e must overcome hate
We must overcome violence
We must overcome greed
We must overcome fighting
We must overcome cruelty

We must overcome all that
tears people apart
and concentrate on all that
brings people together

The Fight

The heart wants to love
yet we hate
The heart wants to understand
yet we are confused
The heart wants equality
  yet we try to dominate one another
The heart wants peace
yet we fight
The heart wants to give
yet we are greedy
The heart wants to help
yet we destroy
The heart wants to care
yet we are insensitive
If only the heart
were a little stronger

We Know Better,
All Women Are One

I am a woman like you are
I am a mother like you are
I am a worker like you are
I am an inamorata like you are
Yet because you live there
and I live here
or because your appearance or lifestyle
is different from mine
people tell us we are not alike
But we can see the differences
in each other's beliefs because
our intrinsic ideals are the same
People tell us we are not alike but
we know better
We are all one

Celebrate All That Binds Us Together

Celebrate
the budding flowers
the clear blue sky
the deep green forests
the perfect full moon
the twinkling stars
Celebrate
the miracle of a baby
the optimism of children
the laughter of adolescents
the responsibility of adults
the wisdom of our elders
Celebrate
the love in our hearts
the spirit in our souls
the health of our bodies
Celebrate
all that binds us together
as one

love
English

حُبّ
Arabic

amor
Spanish

miłość
Polish

αγάπη
Greek

sevgi
Turkish

عشق
Farsi and Dari

ЛЮБОВЬ
Russian

Chinese

kaerlighed
Danish

amor
Latin

kärlek
Swedish

स्नेह
Sanskrit

amore
Italian

چاہت
Urdu

אהבה
Hebrew

amour
French

rakastaa
Finnish

liefde
Dutch

مينه
Pashtu

kjærlighet
Norwegian

Japanese

liebe
German

amor
Portuguese

Love Is the Soul of Hearts

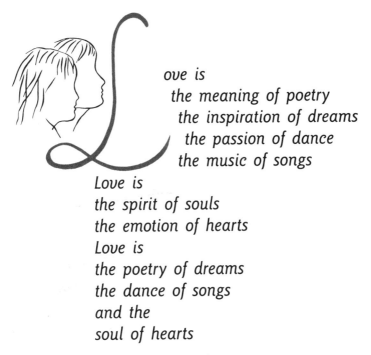

ove is
the meaning of poetry
the inspiration of dreams
the passion of dance
the music of songs

Love is
the spirit of souls
the emotion of hearts
Love is
the poetry of dreams
the dance of songs
and the
soul of hearts

Love

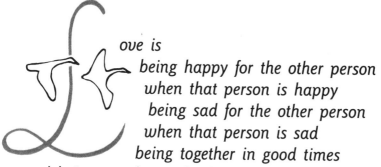

ove is
being happy for the other person
when that person is happy
being sad for the other person
when that person is sad
being together in good times
and being together in bad times
Love is the source of strength

Love is
being honest with yourself at all times
being honest with the other person at all times
telling, listening, respecting the truth
and never pretending
Love is the source of reality

Love is
an understanding so complete that
you feel as if you are a part of the other person
accepting that person just the way he or she is
and not trying to change each other to be something else
Love is the source of unity

Love is
the freedom to pursue your own desires
while sharing your experiences with the other person
the growth of one individual alongside of
and together with the growth of another individual
Love is the source of success

Love is
  the excitement of planning things together
  the excitement of doing things together
Love is the source of the future

Love is
  the fury of the storm
  the calm in the rainbow
Love is the source of passion

Love is
  giving and taking in a daily situation
  being patient with each other's needs and desires
Love is the source of sharing

Love is
  knowing that the other person
  will always be with you regardless of what happens
  missing the other person when he or she is away
  but remaining near in heart at all times
Love is the source of security

Love is the
  source of life

All Mothers Are Sisters,
All Fathers Are Brothers
and All Children Are One

When you interact with children
you must always keep in mind
that everything you do and say
has an enormous impact on their lives
If you treat children
with love and respect
it will be easier for them
to love and respect themselves and others
If you treat children
with freedom and honesty
it will be easier for them
to develop confidence in their
abilities to make decisions
If you treat children
with intelligence and sensitivity
it will be easier for them
to understand the world
If you treat children
with happiness, kindness and gentleness
it will be easier for them
to develop into adults capable
of enjoying all the beautiful things
in life

We Must Learn to Understand One Another

Conflicts always occur
It is in the resolution of conflicts
that human beings stand out
Every conflict can and should be calmed
by talking about and understanding
one another's needs
and by acting with compassion
to solve the differences
This is how all people should get along
This is how we must get along

eople are only complete
when they have a true friend
to understand them
to share all their
passions and sorrows with and
to stand by them
throughout their lives

 friend is
someone who is concerned
with everything you do

A friend is
someone to call upon
during good and bad times

A friend is
someone who understands
whatever you do

A friend is
someone who tells you
the truth about yourself

A friend is
someone who knows
what you are going through
at all times

A friend is
someone who does not
compete with you

A friend is
someone who is genuinely happy
for you when things go well

A friend is
someone who tries to
cheer you up when
things don't go well

A friend is
an extension of yourself
without which
you are not complete

Music transcends barriers
among people
Slow, soft songs
  eyes are sad and misty
Fast songs
  eyes are sparkling
Old familiar songs
  eyes are dreamy
Witty songs
  eyes are laughing
Religious songs
  eyes are wistful

When listening to our own music
we are all one

Let Everyone Sing in Harmony

I see the hurt in your eyes
I see the joy in your eyes
I see the fear in your eyes
We have the same laughter and tears

I smell the beautiful rose
I smell the crisp, clear air
I smell the autumn leaves
Nature's magnificent aromas are the same
    all over the world

I hear the songs of birds
I hear the violins in the symphony
I hear the solitude of death
I hear the laughter of children playing
We all listen to the same sounds

All Hearts Must Be One

Everyone has the same emotions
Everyone has the same feelings
Everyone has the same desires
No matter where we live
or what we believe in
all hearts must be one

We must make the world
a place where
love dominates our hearts
nature sets the standard for beauty
simplicity and honesty are
    the essence of our relationships
kindness guides our actions
and everyone respects one another

One sun
One moon

One world
One heart

ABOUT THE AUTHORS

Susan Polis Schutz grew up in the small country town of Peekskill, New York, where at the age of seven, she first began to write poetry as a means of expressing and understanding her feelings. She graduated from Rider University, majoring in English and biology, and was later awarded an honorary Doctor of Laws degree from that same university. Susan has always found that through writing, she brings clarity to her thoughts and life, and so, following the tragic events of September 11, 2001, it was only natural for her to seek answers in her own writing.

Stephen Schutz, a native New Yorker, spent his early years studying drawing and lettering as a student at the High School of Music and Art in New York City. He received his undergraduate degree in physics at M.I.T. and a doctoral degree in theoretical physics at Princeton University. He developed a popular World Wide Web site, bluemountain.com, where Internet users can personalize and electronically send interactive, animated greeting cards to other users all over the world.

Susan and Stephen moved to Colorado shortly after they were married in 1969. There they decided that they did not like being separated during the workday and wanted to spend all their time together. So they packed their pickup-truck camper with the silk-screened posters composed of Susan's poetry and Stephen's artwork, which they made in their basement. They began a year of traveling together in the camper and selling their posters in towns and cities across the country. In their travels, they found that people everywhere shared their same thoughts and emotions about love, family, and friends. And now, in 2001, Susan and Stephen continue to help people around the world communicate.

In 1972, their first book, **Come Into the Mountains, Dear Friend**, was published. Since then Susan and Stephen have authored many bestselling books of poetry, including **To My Daughter, with Love, on the Important Things in Life**, which has sold over 2½ million copies, as well as **To My Son with Love** and **I Love You**. Susan's poems and Stephen's artwork have been published on over 350 million greeting cards, which are sold and available in many countries in a variety of languages.

By distributing this book free throughout the world, we hope that Susan's words can touch the hearts and lives of people in every country, in every culture... bringing them together in an atmosphere of love and peace.